Black is Beautiful

Edited by Lacey Belinda Smith

John Stewart Rock (1825 – 1866) was an American teacher, doctor, dentist, lawyer and abolitionist. He was one of the first African-American men to earn a medical degree, and he was the first Black person to be admitted to the bar of the Supreme Court of the United States.

Traditionally, Rock is associated with the coining of the term "Black is beautiful" although the historical record does not support that.

Musicians, Tomb of Nakht

Kemsit, Nubian Queen of Kemet Pharaoh Mentuhotep II
(2061-2010 B.C.)

Queen Kemsit having her hair beautified by her
servants. The painting is from her tomb chamber wall –
Metropolitan Museum of Art, NYC.

Modern Nubian girls of Egypt

Black is Beautiful Movement

In 1962, Steven Biko chalenged the world by expressing his thoughts about beauty within the Black community with Black Consciousness in South Africa through his writings. "Man, you are okay as you are, begin to look upon yourself as a human being"—Black is Beautiful.

Caribbean Woman, or *Female Nude with Sunflowers*; Paul Gauguin—1889,
Cloisonnism , Breton period

The Negro Master of the Hounds, Jean-Leon Gerome, Orientalism

Study of Negro, Theodore Chasseriau –1838, Romanticism

Head of a Negro, John Singleton Copley –1778, Neoclassicism

Espejo Negro, Manuel Alvarez Bravo--1947

Resting Negro. Marrakesh, Zinaida Serebriakova –1928, Art Deco

Veronique Boubane, a beauty from Senegal, was a finalist in the 2008 Miss Belgium pageant and now works as a model.

Veronique Boubane and her husband

Virginie Detry

In modern times, Black women have chosen to adapt to Western society and their hairstyles or go for a more natural look. Hair straightening was heavily facilitated by Garrett Augustus Morgan, Sr. and Sarah Breedlove.

Garrett Augustus Morgan, Sr. (1877 – 1963) was an African-American inventor and community leader. His most notable inventions included a revamped sewing machine, a respiratory hood to protect against smoke and a semaphore--a type of traffic signal. He also invented chemicals for straightening hair.

Sarah Breedlove (1867 – 1919), known as Madam C. J. Walker, was an African American entrepreneur, philanthropist, and the first female self-made millionaire in America. She made her fortune by developing and marketing a line of beauty and hair products for Black women through her company Madame C.J. Walker Manufacturing Company.

Hair straightening became very popular among Black males and females of all races, during the 1950s. During the late sixties, the "Afro" and more traditional ways of wearing the hair were in fashion. It went along with the 'Black is beautiful' movement. Today most Black women have chosen to straighten their hair and some going as far as 'Black girl long hair' that reflects societal views of beautiful hair.

Still there is the more natural look.

Beauty pageant contestants

JANELLE COMMISSIONG, 1977

In 1977, Janelle Commissiong won the title of Miss Trinidad and Tobago, and went on to become the first Black Miss Universe in the history of the competition.

Ariana Miyamoto was crowned Miss Universe Japan for 2015. She is Afro-Asian and the first mixed-race woman to be Miss Japan.

Tatiana Silva Braga Tavares, a model of Cape Verdean descent, was crowned Miss Belgium in 2005. She is the First Black woman to win the crown of Miss Belgium.

Laura Beyne, a 19 year old girl from Brussels, became the second Black Miss Belgium in 2012. Her father is Belgian, and her mother Congolese.

Sonia Rolland was born in Kigali, Rwanda. She is a French actress. She was selected Miss France in the year 2000. Her father is French, and her mother Rwandan.

Malou Hansson (born in 1983 in Järfälla, Uppland, Sweden) served as Miss Sweden in 2002. She was the first Black woman to hold this beauty pageant title. Her father was from Sweden and her mother from Ghana.

Iman Kerigo, crowned Miss Norway in 2011. She was born in Kenia, raised in Norway. She was the first woman of African descent to hold the title. Kerigo and her family are refugees from Kenya.

Miss Angola Leila Lopes is crowned by Miss Universe 2011.

www.ingramcontent.com/pod-product-compliance
Lightning Source LLC
Chambersburg PA
CBHW041506280526
45792CB00004B/1150